Gallery Books
Editor: Peter Fallon

GOD'S GIFT

John Banville

GOD'S GIFT

a version of Amphitryon
by Heinrich von Kleist

Gallery Books

God's Gift
is first published
simultaneously in paperback
and in a clothbound edition
on the day of its première,
12 October 2000.

The Gallery Press
Loughcrew
Oldcastle
County Meath
Ireland

© John Banville 2000

The right of John Banville
to be identified as the Author
of this work has been asserted
in accordance with the Copyright,
Designs and Patents Act 1988.

ISBN 1 85235 280 9 (*paperback*)
    1 85235 281 7 (*clothbound*)

    The Gallery Press acknowledges the financial assistance of
An Chomhairle Ealaíon / The Arts Council, Ireland, and the Arts
Council of Northern Ireland.

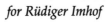

for Rüdiger Imhof

Characters

GENERAL ASHBURNINGHAM
MINNA, his wife
SOUSE, the General's manservant
KITTY, his wife
JUPITER, in the form of Ashburningham
MERCURY, in the form of Souse

Setting

Ireland, summer, 1798

God's Gift was first produced by Barabbas . . . the company, in association with the Eircom Dublin Theatre Festival, at the O'Reilly Theatre, Belvedere College, on 12 October 2000, with the following cast:

ASHBURNINGHAM	Paul Meade
MINNA	Mary O'Driscoll
SOUSE	Raymond Keane
KITTY	Lynn Cahill
JUPITER	Mikel Murfi
MERCURY	Louis Lovett

Director	Veronica Coburn
Producer	Enid Reid Whyte
Assistant producer	Amy O'Hanlon
Designer	Feargal Doyle
Lighting designer	Mark Galione
Costume designer	Kathy Kavanagh
Production manager	Marie Tierney
Stage director	Miriam Duffy
Stage manager	Eimer Murphy

ACT ONE

Scene One

Forecourt of Ashburningham House. The gloom before dawn. Enter SOUSE, *with a lantern.*

SOUSE O God! Who's there? Come out and show
    yourself!
There's no one, seemingly, and yet I thought —
It must have been the wind among the leaves.
This endless night is playing tricks on me.
My head is addled, and I'm seeing things.
An hour ago, or more, the dawn came up:
The sun appeared, and then went down again,
As if some hand had pulled it by a string!
Now my poor lamp is nearly out of oil.
But here's the house, and here's the courtyard,
    too.
There's not a window lit, all still asleep —
Hold up, I see a candle flickering;
(*He counts the windows*) One two, three four: it's
    Lady Minna's room.
She's sleepless, pining for her man. O my!
I could dress up as him, and slip in there,
Between those nice warm sheets, and comfort
    her —
(*Mimics his master's voice*) 'By Jupiter, my dear,
    I've missed you sore!'
(*Mimics* MINNA's *voice*) 'O darling! my divine
    one! sore's the word!'
Go easy, Souse, keep thoughts like that at bay,
Unless you want a hiding, for I swear,
Sometimes I think the Boss can read my mind.
I don't know why he had to send me here,
At night, along these roads, with rebels out

11

In search of heads to stick up on their pikes.
'Go home,' says he, 'go home and tell my wife,
The war is won — the so-called war, that is —
That Vinegar Hill runs red with rebel blood,
That Boolavogue is burning, and that at
The Harrow their "brave" Father Murphy fled.
Describe it all,' he tells me, 'say how well
We fought, and how we held the day against
That pack of rabble!' Oh, I'm sure they did,
I'm sure the Redcoats didn't give an inch,
Though all they had were muskets and the odd
Fourteen-inch cannon, while the other side
Were armed up to the teeth with pikes and
    sticks.
Oh yes, no doubt it was a splendid sight,
And one I would have seen, if I had thought
To put my head out of the Boss's tent,
Where I was in a struggle of my own,
Attacking that fine ham the Boss had left
Unguarded when he went to face the foe.
Begob, that was a skirmish — but hold hard!
There's someone there! — there is! — O, holy
    God!

    Enter MERCURY, *in the form of* SOUSE.

MERCURY (*Aside*) I'd better get this day begun, or else
    Their little world will be all out of tune;
    (*Sarcastic*) It's usually so harmonious.
SOUSE You there!
MERCURY   Who's this? Of course, it would be
    him.
    I'd better get the rascal out of here,
    Before he wakes the household up —
    (*To* SOUSE) Well, friend?
SOUSE (*Aside*) Who is it, who? I seem to know his face.
    I hope he's not a rebel, or I'm caught.
    It's said they save the worst deaths for their
    own.

They nailed old Michael Murphy to his barn,
And burned the house, with Michael's wife
    inside,
And all because they sold the Brits a horse.
What would they do to me, the Boss's man,
His footman, aide-de-camp, and major-domo,
And me an Irishman, an Oylegate Souse!

MERCURY Step forward, there, identify yourself!

SOUSE I'm Souse, the name is Souse, that's Souse, my
    name —

MERCURY You're *who*?

SOUSE   It's Souse, sir, S-o-u-s-e —

MERCURY You're not.

SOUSE   I'm not?

MERCURY   That's what I said —
I'm Souse.

SOUSE You're Souse? (*Aside*) He's Souse. (*To* MERCURY)
    Well, that makes two of us.

MERCURY And how dare you assume my name?

SOUSE   I don't.
I don't assume it. Blame my father for't.
He was a Souse, from out beyond Oylegate;
When I was born, he looked at me and said,
'He shall be callèd Souse, this I decree!'
That's how it goes, in these parts, friend, you
    see:
The father gives the son his name —

MERCURY *strikes him on the ear.*

                         Oo!
Ow!
By Heaven, sir, you pack a mighty punch.

MERCURY Believe me, clown, that was the merest tap.
You see my staff? This staff, you see it, yes?

SOUSE Now listen, man, just take it easy, right?
Put up your stave —

MERCURY   I'll put it up, all right —
In such a way to give you some backbone.

13

SOUSE Oh, charming, charming — lovely talk, I'm
    sure.
    May I go past? I have a message for —
MERCURY You'll go past over my dead body, dog.
SOUSE Look here, let's get this business sorted out.
    My name is Souse —
MERCURY   It's not.
SOUSE   Let's say it is,
    Just for the sake of argument, all right?
MERCURY Who's arguing? You can't be Souse — that's *me*.
SOUSE Then let me put it this way: I was Souse
    Last night, when General Ashburningham,
    Commander of his Royal Majesty's
    Fifteenth Brigade of Suffolk Musketeers,
    And victor of the battle of Vinegar Hill,
    And master of this house, sent me home here,
    His loyal servant, with a message for
    His missus, Lady Minna, telling her
    The war is won, and he's on his way home,
    And would she please arrange a splendid feast,
    And while she's at it, give old Souse a bite,
    And maybe let him have a cup of grog,
    For he's wore out, and hungry as a hog.
MERCURY Now listen, fellow, how you know these things,
    And where you came by so much information,
    I can't begin to guess; but all you say
    Is true, and it all happened — yesterday.
SOUSE It did?
MERCURY   It did. The General sent me here
    To tell my Lady Minna the good news —
    I came; I told her; she was overjoyed.
    Last evening the General arrived,
    The house was given over to a feast,
    And then the happy pair went off to bed,
    Where they are still, and where the General
    Is no doubt even now regaling her
    With details of his battle strategy.
SOUSE (*Aside*) Good God above, am I losing my mind?
    The fellow looks like me, and sounds like me;

But if he *is* me, who the hell am I?
I'll put him to the test. (*To* MERCURY) Tell me,
   my friend,
What present did the General bring home
For Lady Minna?

MERCURY   Why, a silver brooch,
Of Irish silver, with his own initial,
A fancy *A*, engraved in gold upon't.

SOUSE (*Aside*) Damn me, he's right! Let's see, I'll try
   again.
(*To* MERCURY) All right, then, so-called Souse,
   riddle me this:
What were you up to when the fight was on?

MERCURY Inside the General's tent I found a ham —

SOUSE (*Aside*) Begob!

MERCURY   And found a bottle, too, of
   wine,
The General had not had time to drink.
A tasty lunch I had of it —

SOUSE   All right!
No more; I am convinced. But tell me this:
If I'm not Souse, who *is* it that I am?

MERCURY I'm sure I've no idea. Tell you what:
When I'm no longer Souse, you can be him.

SOUSE I can?

MERCURY   Feel free; I give you leave.

SOUSE   Oh, thanks.
That's fair enough. A sound arrangement. Yes.
Only —

MERCURY   What now?

SOUSE   Oh, nothing, nothing.

MERCURY Good.

SOUSE So I'll be on my way, then.

MERCURY   'Bye.

SOUSE   Goodbye.

He makes to go toward the house.

MERCURY Where do you think you're going?

SOUSE   To the
            house.
MERCURY   Have you been listening to me? The house
            Is out of bounds to you while I'm still here.
            If you don't want my staff across your back
            Again you'd better get off quick.
SOUSE   And get
            Off quick to where, exactly, may I ask?
MERCURY   To Hades, if you like.
SOUSE   To *where*?

            MERCURY *strikes him with his staff.*

MERCURY   To Hell!

            SOUSE *flees.*

Dear me, I thought he'd never go! And now —

Checking himself, he turns to the audience.

But you must all be thoroughly confused;
Let me explain. My name is Mercury;
I mean, that is the name men call me by.
You see my magic staff, my golden helm —
But no, of course: you're mortals, therefore
      blind.
You'll have to take my word for all of this.
I am the god of twilight and the wind,
The god of storm, and of the dawn, the god
Of eloquence, of travellers; I am
The god whose task it is to lead
The souls of mortals to the underworld,
The god of commerce, and of games of chance,
The indefatigable messenger
Who brings the news from Heaven down to
      earth.
Today I am about a baser task.
My father, Jupiter, the god of gods,

I blush to say, is up to his old tricks.
Yes, it's a girl again: the Lady Minna.
He saw her out on horseback yesterday,
When he was on his way to view the war —
He loves to watch them fight — and that was
    it;
Knowing that her husband, General
Ashburningham, was otherwise engaged,
He took his form, while I took that of Souse —
Are you still with me? Yes? — and down we
    came.
Poor Minna was completely fooled, of
    course,
Believing that her husband had come home.
All night they have been at it. I, meanwhile,
Am sent out here, to keep the dawn at bay;
Hot Phoebus held his horses these three hours,
To give the old boy time to catch his breath.
It's squalid, certainly, I quite agree;
You'd think that at his age he'd have some
    sense,
And give up girls, and stick to thunderbolts,
And making things go wrong down here on
    earth.
Can't see, myself, what the attraction is.
Young Ganydeme, now, that's another thing —
But wait, here come more mortals — and
    my Dad.

Scene Two

MERCURY *makes a sweeping gesture with his staff, a cardboard sun pops into the sky and the stage is flooded with a golden light; enter* JUPITER *in the form of* ASHBURNINGHAM, *with* MINNA *on his arm, and* KITTY *behind;* MERCURY *becomes invisible.*

JUPITER Well, madam, wasn't that a night?
MINNA   Divine!
         I prayed to Heaven it would never end.
JUPITER And Heaven heard you, dear, I'm sure of it.
MINNA Oh, Kitty, please, bring out my parasol.
KITTY I will, ma'am, sure. (*Aside*) I'd need a shade,
         myself,
         This sun's so hot, and daybreak only broke.

          Exit.

JUPITER Look, love, the dawn has come, the sun is up,
         And though it shines upon a fairer bloom
         Than ever grew upon Olympus' slopes,
         It would be better were it not so bright.
MINNA How so?
JUPITER   I feel — how shall I say? — exposed.
         These hours that we have shared together,
         love,
         Were stolen from my duties at the front.
         It would look bad, if it should get about
         That I had sneaked off home to see my
         wife —
MINNA Sneaked off!
JUPITER   Oh, come now, you know what
         I mean!
         It would be better if my visit here
         Were kept a secret between you and me.
MINNA Does this mean that you're leaving me again?

Enter KITTY *with parasol, raises it, hands it*
to MINNA.

How burdensome your soldier's duties are.
This silver brooch, the precious gift you brought,
I'd give it for a bunch of violets
If you could stay and gather them with me.
You cannot know how dull my life is here,
How empty seems our house, how long the
    days.
Of course, this uprising must be put down,
But, oh, I worry, darling, when I think
Of how much danger you must face each day.
Is one short night to be my recompense
For these past months of torment and of fear?

JUPITER My darling girl, how beautiful you are,
And how your words fall heavy on my heart!
Yes, I must go, there's no avoiding it,
But ere I go, there's something I must say.
I know that by the marriage vows you swore,
You are compelled to love me —

MINNA   What!
    Compelled?

JUPITER I mean you have a duty to love me,
A duty under law, so that I could,
If I were minded to, go to a judge
And make you grant me my conjugal rights.

MINNA What an extraordinary thing to say!
Conjugal rights? My duty under law?

JUPITER But yet it's true, and this is what irks me.
Call it mere foolishness, but there you are.
Think how much better it would be, my dear,
If laws and marriage vows were set at nought
And you should freely offer me your love
Without formality.

MINNA   Formality?

JUPITER Come, speak from out your secret heart and
    say
Whether it was your husband that last night

19

	Brought you such joy, or if it was instead
	The lover, whom the husband's form conceals?
MINNA	Dear heart, I must confess you're baffling me.
	Husband and lover, they are both the same,
	United in your sole belovèd form.
	And as for laws, do they not rather spur
	Us on to bolder feats of love, deeper
	Depths of uncontrolled desire?
	Is passion's pleasure not pricked up by rules?
MERCURY	(*Aside, pretending shock*) Well, madam!
JUPITER	Dear,
	the love I feel for you
	Is greater than what any husband could —
MINNA	But are you not my husband?
JUPITER	Yes, of course!
	But when I hear you say the very word,
	It makes me think of lawyers and of priests,
	All that formality that rings us round.
	It makes it seem that last night in your bed
	The one whom you held in your loving arms
	Was just that ordinary mortal man
	Who led you to the altar, and who thinks
	He has a legal right to all your charms.
	What is he, but a soldier, yes, a lout —
MINNA	A *lout*?
JUPITER	When he's mere husband to you, yes.
MINNA	To me, my darling, you are never *mere*.
JUPITER	Last night — you said yourself — it was
	divine.
MINNA	And so it was.
MERCURY	(*Aside*) I'll *bet* it was.
JUPITER	My dear,
	I wanted to appear in my own being,
	Not in the guise of husband; do you see?
MERCURY	(*Aside*) Oh, here we go: love me, love my
	godhead.
JUPITER	In me are things only a god can know.
	There is a loneliness, a solitude,
	No mortal could endure.

MINNA   Oh, love —

JUPITER   No,
         please,
         Just listen. When I came to you last night,
         As usual the others laughed and said
         Behind their hands, 'Oh, there he goes again,
         Insatiable old goat — '

MINNA   The others — ?
         Goat — ?

JUPITER I mean the other — officers, of course;
         You know how soldiers talk.

MINNA   I certainly
         Do not!

JUPITER   But what they cannot understand
         Is this deep emptiness within my heart
         That I must seek to fill, with human love.
         I'm growing old —

MINNA   You're not yet thirty-five.

JUPITER I mean my heart is old. I'm grey inside;
         The weariness of being who I am,
         You cannot know.

MINNA   I'm younger than you, yes,
         But not by all that much! A mere ten years.

JUPITER Please promise me, my love, that this long
              night
         That we have spent together will not fade;
         That you will keep the memory of it
         As fresh within your breast as if it were
         A night you spent in Heaven —

MINNA   Yes, of course.

JUPITER And that this day that's starting now will be
         A day out of your days, a golden day,
         The light of which will burn throughout your
              life.

MINNA   What can I say?

JUPITER   Say that you promise.

MINNA   Yes,
         I promise.

MERCURY (Aside; sarcastic) Ahh —

21

JUPITER   And when
         Ashburningham
         Returns, still you will think of me as *me*,
         And not as him. You'll promise that, as well?
MINNA When you return, who will you be but you?
         What other you is there that I might love?
         I wish, my dear, you'd stop these riddles now.
JUPITER I will; I'll go; you've promised. Duty calls.
MINNA Oh, how I hate for this brief time to end.
JUPITER Did last night seem more brief than other
         nights?
MINNA Oh no, I meant —
JUPITER   The dawn could do no more
         Than wait upon our happiness this long.
         Day must begin, and men must have their
         light —
         Farewell.

         He becomes invisible.

MINNA   He's drunk on love, and so am I.

         Exit, with KITTY *following; when they are gone,
         all of* JUPITER's *energy drains from him, and he
         sinks down on a grassy mound, exhausted, and
         falls into a doze.*

MERCURY He's not the god he was, and that's the truth.
         The fighting gets him going, fires his blood.
         He loves to see them at each other's throats.
         'Come on,' he'll say to me, 'my little ones' —
         That's what he calls these mortals — 'look at
         them,
         They're buckling on their swords again, let's
         go!'
         Of course, it's not the soldiers interest him;
         No, it's the womenfolk they leave at home.
         He'll watch some swordplay, and some
         skewerings,

	And then, disguised, he'll fly behind the lines,
	Find some incipient widow, and —
JUPITER	(*In his sleep*) My love!
MERCURY	You should have seen him at Thermopylae,
	With young Leonidas's wife.
JUPITER	(*Asleep*) Ah, ah — !
MERCURY	And there was Troy — don't talk to me of Troy.
	If poor old Menelaus only knew
	What Mrs Menelaus — Helen, yes —
	Got up to with (*Jerks thumb toward* JUPITER)
	the old boy here, well now —
	He used to dress up as a eunuch slave,
	And when she took her bath in ass's milk,
	He'd —
JUPITER	(*Cries out in his sleep*) Love me! I will forfeit all
	my strength!
MERCURY	Well, anyway, if Menelaus knew,
	He'd have waged war on Heaven, sure as Hell.

MERCURY *kneels by* JUPITER, *shakes him.*

	Come on now, Dad, it's getting on for noon.
	Let's go and see the rebels being flogged,
	And hear the old triangle jingle-jangle.
	(*Temptingly, trying to wake him*) There'll
	probably be pitchcappings, as well;
	And no doubt hangings, drawings, quarter-
	ings;
	All kinds of human sport. Come on, wake up!
JUPITER	(*Waking; groggily*) Her hands, her beating
	heart, her face on mine —
MERCURY	(*Aside*) It's not enough for him to do it, no,
	He must tell me about it afterwards,
	In quite revolting detail, blow by blow.
	(*Aloud*) Come on, now, Father, let's up and
	away.
	Why don't we go to Egypt?
JUPITER	Egypt?
MERCURY	Yes.

23

Napoleon's going to fight the Mamelukes.
We'll watch a bit of that, bound to be good —
You know what Mamelukes are like — then back
To Paris, and poor lonely Josephine —

JUPITER (*Pushing him away*) Step back, step back, you're blocking out the light —
Napoleon, and Mamelukes — what rot
You talk. Is everything put back in place?

MERCURY Of course.

JUPITER The time adjusted, clocks re-set?

MERCURY I had to strangle a few cockerels —

JUPITER You *what*?

MERCURY A joke.

JUPITER But not a funny one.
Go back and check that nothing's left undone.
That time when we were in Pompeii —

MERCURY Oh,
You always, *always*, have to mention that.
The fact is, if you hadn't overslept,
That girl would not have seen your thunderbolts
Under the bed —

JUPITER (*Loud*) And if you'd not forgot
To hold the dawn another hour —

MERCURY (*Louder*) And
If you'd got out before she woke —

JUPITER (*Loudest*) THERE
WOULD HAVE BEEN NO NEED TO
MAKE VESUVIUS ERUPT!

Pause.

Now please, do as I say.

MERCURY All right!

He makes to go, but lingers; JUPITER *stands brooding.*

24

JUPITER (*Aside*) And yet I cannot go, without her love.
I don't know what's come over me, this time.
The others I could love and leave, not her.
What a predicament it is I'm in:
The mortals look for love to make them gods,
While I'd relinquish my divinity
If she could love me as she loves that
    (*disgustedly*) man.

MERCURY (*Aside*) He'll let them bring us to their level yet.
Does he not understand what is at stake?
These mortals become gods, when they're in
    love,
And where does that leave *us*, I'd like to know.

Scene Three

Before Ashburningham House; KITTY, *with Lady Minna's parasol.*

KITTY   Now, wasn't that the height of tenderness!
      The way they gazed into each other's eyes,
      Oh, that would make a woman feel she's
         loved!
      The General came home for just one night —
      And didn't get a wink of sleep, I'm sure.

Enter MERCURY, *in the form of* SOUSE.

      But then, he's what you'd call a gentleman,
      (*Loudly*) Unlike some others I could name.
MERCURY   (*Aside, ticking off items on his fingers*) Sun's up,
         day's bright, the clocks I have put back,
      I've even changed the bedsheets on her bed —
KITTY   See what I mean? He's off without a word.

She swings the parasol at his head.

MERCURY   What's that?
KITTY   You could say 'bye, at least.
MERCURY   Goodbye.
KITTY   You've been away three months; for all I knew,
      You might have been dead on the battlefield.
MERCURY   (*Aside*) The battlefield! That's rich. Dead drunk,
         more like.
      (*Aloud*) You need have no fear on that score,
         my love:
      Do you think Souse would risk his skin out
         there,
      Amid the cannon smoke and flashing blades?
KITTY   You were a blade yourself, when first we met.
MERCURY   I was? (*Aside*) What, Souse? A blade? Oh,
         deary me!

KITTY   You used to call me darling, hold my hand —
MERCURY   For God's sake, woman, have a little sense.
           It's late already, and the General
           Is halfway back to camp by now. Goodbye!
KITTY   Oh, shame on you! Have you no word of
              warmth,
           Before you go, for your poor faithful wife?
MERCURY   Now, look here, Katie —
KITTY   What!
MERCURY   *Kitty*, I mean.
           The General and Lady Minna, yes,
           Can act as if they're still on honeymoon,
           But you and I, old girl, now don't you think
           We're past that sort of thing?
KITTY   *What* sort of
              thing?
MERCURY   Oh, love, and kisses, all that kind of tosh.
KITTY   *You* may be past it; certainly, I'm not.
MERCURY   When was the last time you looked in the
              glass?
           Or have you given up consulting it?

           Pause.

KITTY   When I heard you were coming home, last
              night,
           I combed my hair, and put on my blue dress,
           The one you always liked; then you arrived,
           And walked past me, as if I wasn't there.
           Do you know how it feels, to be ignored?
MERCURY   The point is, wife, there's nothing you can do
           About the dress that Nature gave to you;
           If you could take *that* off, there'd be some hope
           A man might notice you.
KITTY   In the old days
           That was the *only* dress you liked me in.
MERCURY   That suit has seen too many birthdays, dear.
KITTY   You don't deserve a faithful wife, you pig!
MERCURY   If I'm a pig, then what does that make you?

KITTY The men I could have had! *Real* men, at that.

MERCURY Oh, yes? And who might they have been?
(*Aside*) This will be good: a list of suitors, yet!

KITTY I never gave you cause for jealousy.

MERCURY What, jealous? I? Of you? Don't make me
    laugh.
And no more, please, about how virtuous
You are; virtue is no great thing to us.
Half of our time we spend in schemes
To fool some girl — or, for that matter, boy —
To let us have our way with them —

KITTY   Who's
'us'?

MERCURY The milit'ry, I mean, of course, who else?

KITTY So you're a military man now, eh?
I thought you didn't fancy fighting.

MERCURY   No;
But fighting's not the only thing they do,
Those soldier laddies. Anyway, my dear,
A bit of peace and quiet any day
I'd rather have, than all your purity.
My motto is: Be virtuous if you like,
But just don't preach about it. Now, I'm off!

He becomes invisible.

KITTY (*Looking about*) He's disappeared again; he's
    good at that.
To think, I threw my life away on him!
'Twould serve him right, if I was to take up
With someone else — a rebel fighter, say,
One of those croppies, with his sword and
    pike.
I'd show him, then, what jealousy is like.

Exit.

Scene Four

Enter GENERAL ASHBURNINGHAM *and* SOUSE; MERCURY *invisible.*

ASHBURNINGHAM By Heaven, dolt, I swear I'll break your head
                If you continue with this rigmarole.

SOUSE All I can say is what I know I saw.

ASHBURNINGHAM All you can — all you — what? Now listen,
                Souse,
                I'll calm myself, and hear the whole thing
                  through
                Again.

SOUSE   I told you —

ASHBURNINGHAM   And I'm telling you:
                Tell me again. I'll ask you, point by point —

SOUSE By point, that's good, yes, that's the way to do't.
                You ask me questions, cross-examine me,
                As if we was in court. A good idea.
                I'm in the witness box, you on the bench.
                All right, m'lud, I'm ready. Fire away.

ASHBURNINGHAM All right, then. When, last night, I ordered
                  you —

SOUSE To set off in the pitch-black night, I went
                By every lane and boreen that I knew,
                Afraid of meeting rebels on the prowl.

                MERCURY *puts* SOUSE *into an instant trance
                and steps into his place.*

MERCURY And as I went, I cursed you in my heart.

ASHBURNINGHAM What's this?

MERCURY   The truth, the way you asked for it,
                Without a lick of varnish. Anyway —

ASHBURNINGHAM Go carefully, my man, I warn you.

MERCURY   That's
                Exactly how I went, believe me, sir,
                And all the while rehearsing in my head

	The speech I would make to your lady wife,
	About the battle and the rebels' rout,
	All that — the things you bade me say to her —
	When I was — interrupted.
ASHBURNINGHAM	Yes, go on.
MERCURY	It gets a little tricky, from here on.

MERCURY *makes himself invisible, releases* SOUSE *from his trance.*

SOUSE	The one who interrupted me was Souse.
ASHBURNINGHAM	God blast your eyes, man! what do you mean: Souse?
	What Souse was this? Some kinsman?
SOUSE	No, oh no.
	When I say Souse, it's me I mean: myself.
ASHBURNINGHAM	(*Aside*) Calm, calm; it was an apoplectic fit
	That killed my father, and his father, too.
	(*Aloud*) Good Souse, explain it to me, if you can,
	How it could be that you could meet yourself.
SOUSE	He looked like me —
ASHBURNINGHAM	You said it was pitch-black.
SOUSE	And had my voice —
ASHBURNINGHAM	That's easy imitated.
SOUSE	And knew things of me only I could know.
ASHBURNINGHAM	Such as?

MERCURY *again takes* SOUSE'*s place.*

MERCURY	He knew about the ham.
ASHBURNINGHAM	The ham?
MERCURY	The one you left unguarded in your tent;
	The one I ate —
ASHBURNINGHAM	You ate my ham?
MERCURY	I did.

ASHBURNINGHAM So that's what happened to it; and I
    thought —
    No matter; right; go on.
MERCURY   The claret, too —
ASHBURNINGHAM You drank the wine as well? Then you *were*
    drunk!
MERCURY No no, I'd slept it off, there in the tent.
    By nightfall I was sober as a judge.

    MERCURY *switches with* SOUSE.

SOUSE I walks up here, along this very path,
    I hears a sound, of someone in the dark,
    I lifts my lantern, thus, and there I am!
    I'm standing in the gate, with stave in hand;
    'What ho!' I says, 'and who are you, my man?'

    Switch.

MERCURY 'I'm Souse,' says I.

    Switch.

SOUSE   'Oh, no you're not,' I says,
    'You can't be Souse, since *I* am Souse — '
ASHBURNINGHAM   Wait, wait —

    Switch.

MERCURY 'What is your business here?' I asked.

    Switch.

SOUSE   I said:
    'I don't see what affair it is of yours,
    But I have come to see my master's wife,
    To tell her of our triumphs in the war.'

    Switch.

MERCURY 'I've done all that already, clown,' I says.
'I came here yesterday and brought that news.'
ASHBURNINGHAM You were here yesterday — ?

Switch.

SOUSE   The day before.
I mean, the day before the day *I* came.
I was already there, a day ahead.
ASHBURNINGHAM (*Aside*) My God, I don't know which of us is
   worse,
Him telling this, or me to listen to't.
(*Aloud*) Is this some kind of game you're
   playing, Souse?
Is there some news from home that is so bad
You cannot bring yourself to tell it straight,
But have to hide it in this rigmarole?
Was there some stranger there, usurping me — ?
(*Aside*) Oh, no, oh, Minna, no, I won't
   believe —
(*Aloud*) Tell me the truth, before I break your
   head:
What was my wife about? What man was there?
SOUSE I didn't see your wife, I'm telling you!
The gate was guarded by another Souse,
And his stout stick. He would not let me in,
But turned me straight away, with threats and
   blows.
ASHBURNINGHAM He came out of the house, you say?
SOUSE   Why, no;
I mean, he *may* have been inside, who knows?
I found him at the gate, standing on guard.

Switch.

MERCURY A very handsome figure he cut, too.

Switch.

ASHBURNINGHAM I cannot listen to this any more.
Go now, and feed and water my poor horse.

Exit SOUSE.

There's one of us is mad; it may be me.
There's only one way to find out — and see,
Here comes my lady wife; I'll find out now
If there have been invaders in the house.

He hesitates.

I want to ask, and yet I would not know;
What if — ? But no, I must not think such
   thoughts.

Scene Five

Enter LADY MINNA *and* KITTY.

MINNA   I must away to church, to say a word
           Of thanks to God — if it be right to say
           Such thanks for such a night as I have had.

KITTY   I'm sure God smiles on love of every kind.

MINNA   I hope so, otherwise I'd have to blush.

She sees ASHBURNINGHAM.

           O God! My darling!

ASHBURNINGHAM   (*Aside*)   Why is she so shocked?

MINNA   So soon returned? I thought —

ASHBURNINGHAM   So soon
           returned?
           So soon, you say? You call three months 'so
              soon'?
           Forgive me, wife, for being so abrupt:
           I had imagined, in my innocence,
           That three months would have seemed no
              short a time.
           For my part, I confess, I found them long.

MINNA   But I don't understand —

ASHBURNINGHAM   And nor do I.
           It seems to me that while I was away
           You did not give the clock a single glance,
           Or sigh in longing for your absent love,
           As I did, deep and often, wife, for you.
           The round of pleasures here at home, no
              doubt,
           Made three months fly as if they were one day.
           So pardon, madam, if I come in haste;
           Perhaps I should away, for three months more,
           Though I'm not sure you'd notice I was gone.

KITTY   (*To* MINNA) Now, madam, keep your calm,

please, keep your calm!

MINNA (*To* ASHBURNINGHAM) My dear, I find it
    difficult to grasp
What grounds you think you have for such
    reproach.
If I seem cold to you, I do not know
What further show of love you could expect.
When in the twilight yesterday you came
So suddenly, and kissed me on the neck —

ASHBURNINGHAM I *what*?

MINNA   I gave you all I had of love,
There, on that couch, in the conservat'ry.
And later, when you held me in your arms,
In bed, in candlelight, I said I hoped
The night would never end. What more, I ask,
Do you expect a wife to give — what more?
If I had more, I'd give it, willingly,
But, love, I gave you everything I had.

ASHBURNINGHAM What are you saying?

MINNA   What is it you ask?
I do not understand. You said yourself
That never had a husband known such joy.
You swore, with such a queer light in your face,
That Jupiter himself had not been loved
By Juno with such passion as I showed.

KITTY (*Aside*) It's true, I heard them at it, so I did.

ASHBURNINGHAM Eternal gods!

MINNA   And then, when dawn came up,
No matter how I begged, you would not stay.
I went back, heavy-hearted, to our bed,
And laid me down, and dreamt — oh, such a
    dream!
We were upon some golden mountaintop,
The two of us, just we, and all around
The air was blue, and endless, and so soft —

ASHBURNINGHAM Perhaps that's it, perhaps it was a dream.
Oh, say it was, my darling, say it was!
It was not I who came to you last night,
But just the image of me, while you slept.

35

We all, sometimes, have dreams like that, you
    know.
There's nothing shameful in it —

MINNA   Shameful!
What!
How can you speak of shame? It was no dream,
As you well know. How dare you mock me
    thus,
And say last night was but a dirty dream?

ASHBURNINGHAM How dare I? Madam, how dare *you*, I say!
At twilight yesterday I came home here,
Crept up behind you, kissed you on the neck,
And on the couch we straight away — ?

MINNA   You
dare
Deny it, do you, that you took with me
All freedoms that a husband could demand,
And more?

KITTY   Tut tut.

ASHBURNINGHAM   You jest!

MINNA   It's you who jest!
And jesting of that kind is coarse and cruel.

ASHBURNINGHAM 'All freedoms that a husband could
    demand':
That's what you said?

MINNA   You make it seem a sin.
That was not how you made it seem last night.
Such liberties you took, my woman's pride
Might have rebelled, but that you spoke of love,
And said that under love all things are pure,
That Eros will forgive the basest acts —

ASHBURNINGHAM That *who* — ?

MINNA   The god of love — have you
forgot?

ASHBURNINGHAM The god of love — Oh, Lord in Heaven, help!
Where's Souse? Here, Souse, come here, I need
    you. Souse!

Enter SOUSE *at a run.*

SOUSE	I'm here, my General!
ASHBURNINGHAM	About time, too. Where have you been, you clod? Were you asleep?
SOUSE	I had a little nap, sir, yes, I had.
ASHBURNINGHAM	My wife insists that I was here last night. Please tell her she imagined it.
SOUSE	(*To* MINNA) You did.

Pause.

ASHBURNINGHAM	Well, go on, man! Say where I was. Speak out!
SOUSE	You were at camp, of course, and I was here.
MINNA	Yes, he was here, I saw him.
SOUSE	Did you? Well Now, that's another story. Anyway —
ASHBURNINGHAM	You heard him say it, wife: I was at camp, Not here, in bed with you, and all your charms —
MINNA	Please stop, please stop, I cannot bear it — stop!
SOUSE	(*Aside*) Begob, he has her rightly in a state.
ASHBURNINGHAM	My dearest Minna, please, bethink yourself. If you persist with this wild jest —
MINNA	Wild jest!
ASHBURNINGHAM	There will be evil consequences sure. Tell me what really happened here last night. The truth is best; however hard it is, I'll bear it, and I'll find it in my heart, I'm sure, to pardon you for your mistakes.
MINNA	There's no mistake! Dear God, I'm going mad.
SOUSE	I think she's right there, Boss, she looks half cracked.
ASHBURNINGHAM	Be quiet, you, or I shall have you flogged!
KITTY	And rightly you'd deserve it, too, I say!
SOUSE	(*Aside*) Oh, that's the way: whenever there's a row, Turn on poor Souse, and kick him up the rear.
ASHBURNINGHAM	All right, my dear, I'll calm down, if you will. Now tell me, who else saw me here?

37

MINNA	Who else?
	Are you demanding witnesses of me?
	The servants saw you; Mary-Anne, my maid;
	Old Hanna cooked our dinner, Prunty served;
	The groomsman, that you told to tend your horse;
	All who were in the house and grounds saw you.
	The dogs, the cat, the very floors you walked on,
	All will stand witness for me, if you ask.
KITTY	And I can vouch for every word she says,
	For I was here, sir, truly, that I was!
MINNA	But wait — do you want proof? Decisive proof?
	From where did I receive this silver brooch?
ASHBURNINGHAM	What silver brooch?
MINNA	This one, about my neck.
SOUSE	Ah, hang on, missus, now, that just can't be.
	I have that yoke here, in its casket, sealed.
	The General gave it to me last night,
	To bring to you, announcing his return.
MINNA	*This* silver brooch you have *there*, in that box?
SOUSE	Well, look and see; I'll open it.

He opens the box.

	Oh, Jaze!
	It's empty! But the seal was on it, look!
ASHBURNINGHAM	How can it be?
SOUSE	Now wait, I wonder if —
ASHBURNINGHAM	(*Aside*) This goes from bad to worse; what next, dear Lord?
MINNA	(*To* KITTY) How pale he is, how shocked; what can it mean?
KITTY	It's just some test he's making you go through; If Souse is in on it, I'll box his ears!
SOUSE	(*Whispers, to* ASHBURNINGHAM) I think I have a notion, Boss, what's up.
ASHBURNINGHAM	Well, tell me then, before I lose my wits!

SOUSE	Remember what I told you, how last night
	When I came here I found another Souse?
	Maybe there was another *you*, as well?
ASHBURNINGHAM	I swear it, Souse, if you start that again
	I'll have you pitch-capped. Ghosts I've heard
	of, yes,
	This godforsaken country is all ghosts
	And goblins, and — what is that word?
SOUSE	Pishogues.
ASHBURNINGHAM	And changelings, fairy forts, and all the rest;
	But tell me this, what sort of ghost is it
	That would cuckold a husband?
SOUSE	But that's it!
	That's what I'm telling you — it was *your* ghost!
	I mean your double, just the same as mine.
	I was de-Soused, and *you* de-Generalised!
ASHBURNINGHAM	Are you in this with her? Did she get you
	To make up all this nonsense, to fool me?
SOUSE	I swear upon my mother's grave — !
ASHBURNINGHAM	Be quiet!
	(*To* MINNA) Now listen, dear, please tell me,
	word for word,
	Exactly how it was when I came home.
MINNA	I've told you —
ASHBURNINGHAM	Yes, but tell me it again;
	Describe the day, the weather, how I looked;
	Leave not a single detail out.
MINNA	All right.
	It was at close of day, the sun had set,
	The birds were whistling their last drowsy
	songs,
	And all the world was settling down to rest;
	I had been at my needlework, and now
	I'd fallen into dreaming —
ASHBURNINGHAM	Dreaming, yes.
MINNA	It was a dream of you, and battlefields,
	And guns, and blood, when from the gate I
	heard
	Such shouts of joy, I knew you had come home.

ASHBURNINGHAM And then?

MINNA I felt a shudder in my blood,
And on my neck the breath as of a kiss,
And when I turned, there you were, darling.

ASHBURNINGHAM I?

MINNA Yes, you; who else?

ASHBURNINGHAM What did I say? Go on.

MINNA You said that you had come straight from the
war,
To spend the night with me —

ASHBURNINGHAM The night, with
you?

MINNA We sat down on the couch, and you —

ASHBURNINGHAM I what?

MINNA You put your arm about my waist —

ASHBURNINGHAM Go on.

MINNA And then —

ASHBURNINGHAM And then?

MINNA You were impatient.

ASHBURNINGHAM Yes?

MINNA You said you could not wait for dinnertime;
You said you did not need to eat or drink;
You said I would be food enough for you;
You said you were a god, and I your nymph;
You said — you said —

ASHBURNINGHAM Yes? What more did I
say?

MINNA Why must you make me speak it all again?
I never knew your tongue to be so free,
Your words so sweet, your hands so
gentle —

ASHBURNINGHAM Oh!
(*Aside*) Sweet words, and gentle hands —
but *whose*, my God?
(*Aloud*) Go on, spare me no detail — on, I
say.

MINNA Well, then you took my arm, and I stood up —

ASHBURNINGHAM Stood up.

MINNA And then you led me to the couch —

ASHBURNINGHAM   The couch.
         MINNA   The couch.
ASHBURNINGHAM   The couch.
         SOUSE   The couch.
         KITTY   The couch.
ASHBURNINGHAM   What happened on this couch?
         MINNA   What
                   happened?
ASHBURNINGHAM   Yes.
         MINNA   Well, afterwards —
ASHBURNINGHAM   No no: what happened *before* afterwards?
         MINNA   How can you ask? You *know* what happened.
ASHBURNINGHAM   No!
                   I do not know what happened. Now, go on.
         MINNA   You'd make me say such things aloud? For
                   shame!
ASHBURNINGHAM   For shame? For shame, you say? What
                   brazenness!
                   Last night, did you feel shame, betraying me?
         MINNA   Betraying you — ?
ASHBURNINGHAM   Betrayed me, yes, you did!
                   It was not I who crept in here last night,
                   As you well know; *I* did not kiss your neck,
                   I did not take your hand, whisper sweet words,
                   And all the rest of it.
         MINNA   Oh, this is foul!
                   How can you doubt me? How? After last night,
                   The sweetest night that I have ever known,
                   When after dinner we retired to bed,
                   And lay entwined as one, for hour on hour,
                   And wished the dawn would never come —
ASHBURNINGHAM   Stop! Stop!
                   You are tormenting me! My heart will burst!
                   (*Aside*) Oh, God, how can she be so cruel, how?
                   (*Aloud*) I do not know, love, what it was I did,
                   That you should need to punish me like this.
                   I am a soldier, and my ways are rough,
                   And yet I swear, I'd gouge out both my eyes
                   Before I would offend you knowingly.

41

MINNA I, punish you? It's you who's punished me!
This is some wicked trick you're playing here.
If you've found someone else, then say it out;
At least do me that honour, and don't lie,
And toy with me, and make me seem a fool
Before the world. I would have let you go,
Had you but asked, instead of playing games,
And making sport with me.

ASHBURNINGHAM   I, sport with you?
It was not I you sported with last night,
So shamelessly —

MINNA   Don't say another word!
You are released, I free you from your vows.

KITTY Oh, madam, please, think what you're saying,
please!

ASHBURNINGHAM I see it now, of course: this was your plan,
To cuckold me, and so dishonour me,
That I would have no choice but to withdraw,
And leave you free to wallow in your lust
With this usurper.

MINNA   Oh! you go too far.

ASHBURNINGHAM Too far? You don't know how far I can go.

*He strides to one side, stands in baffled anger,
trying to unravel the mystery in his head.*

MINNA (*Weeps*) Oh, Kitty, Kitty, what is happening?

KITTY God's truth, I don't know, madam.

SOUSE   Well, I
think —

KITTY You shut your mouth, and don't make matters
worse!

MINNA My head is spinning, I must try to think.

She walks to the opposite side of the stage to
ASHBURNINGHAM, *stands weeping quietly.
The mortals are cast into a trance.*

KITTY Well, what a scene (*her voice fading*) —
           that — was —

           JUPITER *and* MERCURY *come forward; they*
           seem exhausted.

MERCURY You see what happens? It's always the same.
           You stoke their passions, spark their jealousy,
           Rekindle love, until they're so alive
           They take on godliness! And us? We fade
           Before their fire like candles in the sun.
JUPITER (*Musing*) Yes, warmth, that's what it is, just
               human warmth,
           That's what we crave, us poor undying ones.
MERCURY Perhaps *you* want to take on mortal form,
           And live as mortals do, and die like them,
           But I, dear Dad, prefer divinity.
           You've had your night with her; now, can we
               go?

           They stand regarding each other.

ACT TWO

Scene One

All exactly as before. Although MERCURY *tries to stop him,* JUPITER *lifts a finger, releasing the mortals from their trance, while he and* MERCURY *become invisible;* MINNA *and* ASHBURNINGHAM *look over their shoulders at each other,* MINNA *tearfully,* ASHBURNINGHAM *furiously; they exit in opposite directions.*

KITTY   Why does he claim
He spent last night in camp, and not with her?

SOUSE Because he did.

KITTY   You're in on it, I knew!

SOUSE And what exactly is it I'm 'in on'?

KITTY It is some filthy trick the two of you
Have thought up to torment that poor dear
     girl.

SOUSE Some trick there is, but I'm not playing it.
(*Aside*) Uh-oh, it just occurs to me to think:
If someone got into the Boss's bed,
Was there a someone too who got in mine?
I don't know if I really want to know.
And yet I can't remain in ignorance.
(*Aloud*) And tell me, Kitty, how are things with
     you?
We've been apart three long and lonely months,
Does that not merit even one small kiss?

KITTY How dare you talk to me like that, you cur!

SOUSE I beg your pardon — what was that you said?

KITTY You heard me.

SOUSE   But I can't believe my ears.
The thing is, wife, I don't know if you've
     heard —
And stop me if you have — but people when
They meet up after being long apart,

They usually say hello, shake hands,
And if they happen to be man and wife,
Why, they might even hug, exchange a kiss,
Say, *Darling, how I missed you!* and so forth.
They do not snarl, and call each other 'cur',
And look as if they've caught a nasty smell.

KITTY I swear, I don't know how I keep myself
From boxing your two ears, and teaching you
To recognise a woman who's been wronged.

SOUSE You have been wronged?

KITTY   Yes, wronged, as
you well know!

SOUSE I only know it's long past breakfast-time.

KITTY You'll get no breakfast here, least not from me,
Until you make me an apology.

SOUSE Apology? For what?

KITTY   For all the things
You said to me last night, again today.

SOUSE What things I said? But listen, Kitty dear —

KITTY Don't you 'dear' me!

SOUSE   I wasn't here last night!
I mean, I was, but you I didn't see.
I came, and someone stopped me at the gate —

KITTY Who stopped you?

SOUSE   Let's leave that for now.
Suffice to say that I was stopped.

KITTY   Then how
Did you get in my lady's room?

SOUSE   I *what*?

KITTY It had struck midnight when I saw you there,
Shutting her door, a finger to your lips.
I'd brought a toddy for her ladyship,
The one she takes to get her off to sleep.
'Don't make a sound,' you said. 'They're both
    in there;
The General has come home suddenly,
And they won't thank you for disturbing
    them.'

SOUSE And what did I do next?

KITTY   Well, you tell me!
I went back to our room, and waited there
For you; an hour passed; I fell asleep;
I woke up with a start; you hadn't come;
I went to look for you, and there you were,
Outside their bedroom still, and fast asleep.
It was the strangest thing I ever saw:
For standing up, you were, your head like this,
And leaning on your staff; I thought at first
You were a statue. And there was a light,
A kind of light that shone out from your face.
And on your ankles and your cap — don't
    laugh —
I thought I saw these little folded wings.
(SOUSE *laughs loudly*) I told you not to laugh.
It's what I saw.

SOUSE Don't be a fool, it's sleepwalking you were.
I never was inside the house last night.

KITTY And then you woke, and looked at me so
    strange,
And lifted up one finger, just like this,
And said nary a word, but only smiled.

Pause. MERCURY *puts* SOUSE *into a trance, steps
forward himself.*

MERCURY A light, you say, a light was in my face?
Did I look like a man, or like a god?

KITTY, *lost in memory of the vision, is not
listening.*

KITTY And then, this morning, oh! the things you
    said.
How could you be so cruel, so unkind?

MERCURY What did I say? In what way was I cruel?

KITTY It's not my fault I'm growing old and plain.
You loved me once; you might respect me
    now.

MERCURY (*Gently*) But how can we respect what we
      have made?
KITTY I swear, I have a mind to make you pay,
      And dearly, for insulting me that way.
MERCURY (*Eagerly*) You'd make me pay? What do you
      mean?
KITTY   I mean,
      As I already said to you today,
      You needn't think you are the only man
      Who has an eye for me.
MERCURY   Oh yes? Go on.
KITTY You mocked me for my virtue; I'll show you
      That two can make a mockery of love.

       MERCURY *switches with* SOUSE.

SOUSE What are you saying? Has that tinker man
      Been sniffing round these parts again? Has he?
KITTY What if he has? What do you care?
SOUSE   I care
      Enough to break your neck if you as much
      As look at him.
KITTY   I might do more than look.
MERCURY (*Aside; almost enviously*) Such passion, even in
      the light relief!

     He fades back into the background, his powers
     faltering before the spectacle of human passion.

SOUSE (*To* KITTY) I'm warning you —
KITTY   Here comes the
      mistress — shush!

Scene Two

Enter LADY MINNA.

MINNA   Oh, Kitty, tell me, what is happening!
        I feel so lost and miserable. Look,
        You see this silver brooch that I have here,
        That General Ashburningham gave me?
        It has his own initial scored in it.

KITTY   Lovely it is, but, madam, I can't see
        The General's initial anywhere.

MINNA   What are you saying, woman? Are you blind?
        There is an *A*, engraved just here.

KITTY   There's not.
        The only letter I can see's a *J*.

MINNA   A *J*?

KITTY   A *J*.

SOUSE   Oh, Jaze! A *J* it is.

MINNA   Oh, don't say so, please don't, or I am lost.

KITTY   Why, what's the matter, ma'am?

SOUSE   (*Aside*)   Now here we
        go,
        Another piece of hocus pocus.

MINNA   How
        Should I explain what I don't understand?
        I went back to my room not knowing if
        I was awake or dreaming, having heard
        My husband say such awful things to me,
        Especially that he believed the man
        Who spent the night with me was not himself
        But some usurper, and I asked myself
        If I was wrong, for one of us must be,
        My husband or myself, and then I thought
        How odd the way the husband last night
          spoke
        About the husband who would come today,
        Who would, he said, be just a mortal man,

	An ordinary soldier, and a lout.
KITTY	A lout? Your husband called himself a lout?
ASHBURNINGHAM	(*Off*) Where are you, Souse! Come, saddle up
	my horse!
MINNA	He said if he were husband only, yes,
	He'd be a lout.
KITTY	But what else could he be?
SOUSE	I'm coming, sir, I'm on my way right now!

*He dithers, torn between obeying an angry
master and hearing the end of* MINNA's *story.*

MINNA	He could be lover, as he'd been last night.
	That's what he said, and seemed to mean it,
	too.
KITTY	But does he think that he's two separate men?
MINNA	I don't know what he thinks. Perhaps he's lost
	His faculties of reasoning and thought.
SOUSE	He's not himself, that's true, I've noticed it.
ASHBURNINGHAM	(*Off*) Get out here, Souse, or else I'll have your
	ears
SOUSE	Directly, sir; I've got your saddle here.
	(*To the women*) It's certainly his voice, I'll vouch
	for that.
KITTY	But had you doubts, before you saw this *J*?
MINNA	Oh, I don't know; my mind is all awhirl.
	The only thing there was I did not doubt,
	The single, solid thing that I could show
	To prove there was no other in my bed,
	Except my husband, was this silver brooch,
	Which he gave me last night with his own
	hands.
	But when I show it in the light of day,
	I find there is no *A* there, but a *J*!
KITTY	But is it possible that you were wrong?
	I mean about the letter, not the man.
MINNA	I cannot have been wrong! It was an *A*!
	But now I look, and see that it's a *J*!
	If I mixed up the letters, could it be

I mixed the men up, too?

SOUSE (*Aside*) I'll kick myself
I didn't have a go at her last night;
She might have taken me for old King George!

Enter ASHBURNINGHAM.

ASHBURNINGHAM You villain, Souse — !

Seeing MINNA, *he pauses; they gaze at each other, he harshly, she pleadingly.*

Where is my saddle,
Souse?
I would be out of here without delay;
The air's turned foul, I would not smell it
longer.

SOUSE Oh, coming, sir, I'll be there straight away.

Exit SOUSE. ASHBURNINGHAM *continues gazing at* MINNA *for a moment, then turns abruptly, exits.*

MINNA Ah, Kitty, how could I mistake that man
For any other? I'd more easily
Mistake myself, think I was someone else,
In spite of knowing that I *must* be me.
Look at this hand, does it belong to me?
This bosom? My reflection in the glass?
For me to mistake him he'd need to be
More strange to me than my own and known
self!
Put out my eye, still I would hear his voice;
Stop up my ears, I would still feel his touch;
Take touch from me, I'd breathe his presence
in;
Take all my senses, only leave my heart,
Its beat would answer to his blood.

KITTY Ah, ma'am,

I'd never doubt it, for indeed, how could
A woman make such a mistake? A dress,
Now, aye, a pot or pan, you might pick up
The wrong one, in a hurry — not a man,
Not even in the darkness of the night,
And he your husband, too! No no, I say,
Some simple explanation there must be
For all this old *rí-rá** and rigmarole.
And anyway, we all saw him last night,
Young Mary-Anne, old Hannah, Prunty, too,
We cheered him at the gate when he rode in,
As large as life, on that big horse of his.

MINNA Yet how did the initial change itself?
It's there; the weakest eye could not but see,
Yet I saw not, or saw it as an *A*.
Oh, Kitty, if I can't tell names apart,
Is it not possible two Generals
There are, and *they* I failed to tell apart?

KITTY Now, my poor child, you must not doubt
     yourself.

MINNA My virtue I don't doubt. My soul is pure.
I've never loved another man save him.
And yet I must confess — it's very strange —
He never seemed so handsome, like a god,
As when he took me in his arms last night.
He seemed a living portrait of himself,
A painting by a master, showing him
Exactly as he is and yet transformed!
Standing there, he was — I don't know what:
A dream; a fantasy; and yet a man.
I felt such happiness, oh, Kitty dear!
A happiness I've never known before.
And love, what love we had — it was such
     bliss.
I would have asked if he had just come down
From out the stars, if it were not the case
That he seemed so already, in my eyes.

---

* pronounced 'ree-raw'

My husband, yet descended from the skies!
KITTY It was your fancy, dear; love has a way
Of making even dolts seem Heaven-born.
Now take my Souse —
MINNA But oh, the way he kept on making jokes,
About the difference between himself
And General Ashburningham —
KITTY   You say
That's what he called himself, in just that way?
MINNA He called himself my lover, and he said
My husband was a dullard, and a lout.
I smiled, as at a joke, but now I think
The joke was one that he had made on me.
KITTY Now, don't torment yourself, and let us
      think:
When you showed him the silver brooch today
He must have seen what the initial was,
And yet he made no protest.
MINNA   But perhaps
His eye passed over it too quickly, and
He did not see it was not *A*, but *J*.
What can I find to say in my defence?
The very silver brooch I showed as proof
That he was here, is now a proof 'gainst *me*!
Where shall I flee, where shall I find to hide
From his hard eyes, who thinks himself
      betrayed?
And even if I swore upon an oath
That it was he who brought the silver brooch,
How would he not distrust me? And indeed,
How would I also not distrust myself?
KITTY Dear madam, calm yourself — for here he
      comes.

Scene Three

JUPITER *makes himself visible, in the form of* ASHBURNINGHAM.

MINNA My darling, you've come back! Thank God for
        that.
JUPITER Come back? Of course I have —
MERCURY (*Aside*) See how her doubt and fear restore his
        strength!
        (*To* KITTY)   You, woman, go.

> KITTY, *startled to be so brusquely addressed,*
> *pretends to leave, but stays in hiding to eaves-*
> *drop.*

MINNA My dearest Percy, take this silver brooch,
        Examine it, and tell me truly if
        It is the one you gave to me last night,
        Although the name that's on it is not yours.
JUPITER My dear —
MINNA   No, take it, look at it, please do!
        For if it was not you who gave me it,
        Then I admit, I have dishonoured you.
JUPITER Dishonoured me? What nonsense you do talk.
MINNA Please, only tell me: was it you or not?
JUPITER Of course it was. Who else would it have been?
        And even if it was another, why,
        You *thought* him me, and therefore me it was.
MINNA It *wasn't* you — that's what I hear you say.
        Oh, God, I cannot bear the shame of it.
        How cruelly deceived I was!
JUPITER   Not you!
MINNA How so?
JUPITER   It was not you who was deceived,
        But *him*. For when he held you in his arms,
        It was your husband's breast you lay upon,
        Not his; and even when he kissed your lips,

It was Ashburningham *you* kissed. Yes yes!
He knows that's how it was, and I don't doubt
That knowledge burns itself into his soul.

MINNA I wish that Heaven's fire would strike me
    down.

JUPITER Be careful Heaven doesn't grant your wish.

MINNA I must go 'way, I'll leave your house at once —

JUPITER Had I the power to cancel all last night —

MINNA Oh, that you had!

JUPITER   I would not do it, dear.

Pause.

What if — let's posit the hypothesis —
What if the man who came to you last night
Was not a man at all?

MINNA   Was not a man?
Is this another joke at my expense?

JUPITER Oh, humour me. Let's say it was — a god.

MINNA A god?

JUPITER   A god; some Roman deity.
Say it was Jupiter himself. You know
How in the stories that you learned at school,
The god of gods would often come to earth
In mortal form to woo a girl he loved.

MINNA (*Aside*) Oh, Kitty, you were right, it is a game
He's playing here, to test me in some way.
Well, two can play at that game.
(*Aloud*)   Pray, go on.

JUPITER If that is who it was — the god, I mean —
Then we must think how honoured we have
    been.

MINNA An honour, sir, to be thus foully tricked?

JUPITER A trick, you say? A god in love plays tricks?
I'd guard my tongue, if I were you, my girl.
Think of Europa, Leda, Callisto,
Those mortal women Jupiter all loved:
Did *they* feel tricked?

MINNA   I'm sure I couldn't say.

Europa rode a bull into the sea,
While Callisto was turned into a bear,
And Leda, she was ravished by a swan.
Would you count such misuses honouring?

JUPITER He gave them immortality.

Pause.

(Aside) The gift
That mortals long for, and the gods abhor.

MINNA And if it were a god, just tell me this:
How could a mortal girl survive such love?
His radiance would have consumed me all;
His beauty would have burned me into dust;
I would have been unmade by his mere touch.

JUPITER Who but a god could have deceived you, dear?
Who else could have upset the finely poised
Gold-balance of your heart, except a god?
Look at the silver brooch: whose name is there?

MINNA I grant you, it is his initial — J.

JUPITER And he alone, bold Jupiter, would have dared
To creep into your bed so fearlessly.
Yet even such a rival I defeat,
For he knew well, if he were to succeed,
In *my* form only could he come to you,
For only *me* would you love with such fire
As last night you loved him.

*He watches her closely, hoping she will deny
what he is saying.*

MINNA *(Still playing the game)* Well said; it's true.
And so you must be right: it was the god.

JUPITER It was.

Pause.

Yet there is something troubling me.

MINNA What's that, my love?

JUPITER	If you offended him.
MINNA	If I — ?
JUPITER	— convincingly acknowledged him?
MINNA	But what more was it that I should have done?
JUPITER	Do you believe in him sufficiently,

And see his glory in this wondrous world,
In heights of sky, and bluest depths of sea,
The sleeping daisy, and the rose unfurled?
For he is in the dawn, and in the dusk,
He's here in summer, and in winter, too,
In seed, in weed, in grain, and in the husk.
He's in all creatures, and he is in *you*.
Does not the cataract announce his name?
Does not the nightingale his praises sing,
The lightning give burnt off'rings to his fame?
Is he not at the heart of everything?
   Creation beats to his unceasing pulse;
   Him only should you love, and no one else.

MINNA How — (*Ironically*) prettily you put it; and
   how true.

JUPITER You mean it? You'll love *him*, and no one else?

MINNA If that is what the god, and you, command.

JUPITER My dear, it's not a matter of command.
   Unless love's given freely, it's not love.

MINNA I swear, if he came here to me again,
   I'd kneel before him, and proclaim my love —

JUPITER I have no doubt he hears you, and is pleased.

MINNA Or should I say, my deepest reverence.
   For *you*, of course, dear heart, have my *true*
   love.

JUPITER (*Aside*) What damned, deluded hope brought
   me back here!
   (*Aloud*) But say, my dear, the god was I, not
   him?

MINNA Then I should wonder where my husband is,
   And I should follow you to Hades, yes,
   Like Eurydice, so he'd rescue me.

She puts her arms around him.

56

JUPITER But what if he were to appear right now?
MINNA How could he, since *you* are already here?
JUPITER But if he did, you'd know it is the god,
And not your husband, you hold in your arms.

She steps back from him abruptly.

MINNA I'd be so sad, and wish *he* were the god,
And you could go on being who you are.
JUPITER (*Aside*) I did not know I had such awesome
power,
To fashion one so faithful and so fair.
I must be reconciled; she won't love me.
(*Aloud*) Well, Minna dear, you've proved your
steadfastness.
I cannot think why I distrusted you.
Come, Souse, come here at once, I need you!

Enter SOUSE.

SOUSE Sir!
JUPITER Go to the village, tell the people there,
Ashburningham invites them to a feast,
To celebrate his homecoming.
SOUSE   At once!

Exit JUPITER *and* MINNA, *arm in arm.*

But hang on there a minute — *all* of them?
Begob, they'll eat him out of house and home.

Scene Four

KITTY steps out of hiding.

KITTY Such blathering as I have never heard!
  A god, indeed; what will he think of next?
  Why can't he just say he was drunk last night,
  Or something similar, and so forgot
  That he was here? — And yet, he spoke so
    fine,
  And looked so fair when he was saying it,
  That for a moment it might seem that he —
  But no; as easy think my Souse a god,
  And, God almighty, look at him, the ass!
  But still, the priests say we are part divine,
  That there's in us a holy light that shines
  Forever, that will never be put out.
  It's there, in lady and in gentleman,
  And even in the lowly ones, like us.
  (*To* SOUSE) Come here and let me look into
    your eyes.
SOUSE How's that?
KITTY   Your eyes — I want to look in
    them.
SOUSE I haven't touched a drop since yesterday.

She holds his head and peers deep into his eyes.

KITTY There *is* a light, I see it glowing there.
SOUSE Let go of me, you madwoman, let go!
  Last night my face was all aglow, you said,
  But now there's only embers in my eyes?
  Before I know it I'll be all burnt out.
  Then, I suppose, you'll get the tinker man
  To warm you up instead.
KITTY   The tinker man?
  Ah, that was just a joke.

SOUSE   Oh, is that so?
        Try joking with me in that way again
        And I'll mend your old kettle, so I will!
KITTY   Can you not rise above yourself at all?
        Can you not find a decent word to say
        To one who's stuck by you for all these years?
SOUSE   Stuck *to* me, like a leech, you mean.
KITTY   That's
            right,
        Insult me, me, who thought you were a god.
SOUSE   A god? Oh, that's the best one I've heard yet.
        And I suppose that you're a goddess, too?
KITTY   Ah, no, I'm only human; but I thought,
        Just for a minute there, I thought you might,
        I thought maybe you might be able to —

        She weeps, and turns aside to hide her tears.
        MERCURY *switches with* SOUSE.

MERCURY You thought I might be able to — ?
KITTY   Love me.
        I mean, like in the old days.
MERCURY   Love you?
KITTY   Yes.
        Is it so much to ask, a little love?

        Pause. He switches back with SOUSE.

SOUSE   The *old* days, were they ever new, for *us*?
        Don't cry, old girl; I'll try to mend my ways.
KITTY   Are you still hungry?
SOUSE   No.
KITTY   There's stirabout,
        And soda bread, and honey in the pot.
SOUSE   I told you, I'm not hungry.

        Pause.

KITTY   (*Tenderly*)   Yes, you are.

59

Scene Five

MERCURY, *on a balcony above.*

MERCURY I hope you know, old Father Jupiter,
The kind of pander you've made of your son.
All night I guarded by her bedroom door,
While you and she within made happy sport.
But what of me? Who cares how I might feel?
I'm only Mercury, the errand boy.
Yet I have loved, more fervently than you,
More daringly — more generously, too.
I loved young Perseus, that golden boy,
And asked for nothing of him, only gave.
That day he fought Medusa, I stepped in,
To guide his sword, and keep his courage up.
And when the fight was done, and he had won,
He turned from me as if I were not there.
You would have used a spell to win his love,
Not I; though I'm the trickster, I don't trick
Where love's concerned —

Enter ASHBURNINGHAM.

But wait, who have
we here?
ASHBURNINGHAM (*Aside*) A silver brooch kept under lock and key
Is somehow stolen, though the seal's intact,
And in its place another one is left —
Oh, well, magicians do it all the time,
It doesn't have to be the work of gods.
To steal a man's own form, though, and thereby
Disguised to steal into his marriage bed,
That's magic, surely, of the blackest sort.
I can't believe my Minna's false; I can't;
Some other explanation there must be.
MERCURY (*Aside*) How sorry for themselves they

	always feel,
	When Dad comes down and pushes them aside.
	Let's rub a grain of salt into the wound.
	(*Aloud*) Hello there, may I help you, friend?
ASHBURNINGHAM	It's me,
	You villain, open up the gate at once.
	I thought you were off saddling up my horse.
MERCURY	I beg your pardon? And just who are you?
ASHBURNINGHAM	Now listen here, I'm in no mood for jokes —
MERCURY	No more am I, so off you go, my man.
ASHBURNINGHAM	Inform my wife that I've returned.
MERCURY	Your wife?
	And who is that? The cook? The chamber maid?
	Or that great fat-arsed one who tends the pigs?
ASHBURNINGHAM	Have you been drinking, man?
MERCURY	You took the words
	Out of my mouth: have *you*?
ASHBURNINGHAM	I'll have you hanged.
MERCURY	I think you would do best to go, my friend.
	This house is General Ashburningham's,
	And I'm his man. The General's within —
ASHBURNINGHAM	He's what? The General is here, you say?
MERCURY	That's right, him and his lady wife —
ASHBURNINGHAM	Oh, God!
MERCURY	I know they wouldn't want to be disturbed,
	While they're enjoying — what'll I say? — a nap.

He makes himself invisible.

Scene Six

ASHBURNINGHAM I feel as if I've died, gone to my grave,
And come back as a ghost. What does it mean?
I don't know what to do. I am undone.
My wife is sleeping with another man,
Who claims he's me, while I stand at my gate.
If I speak out, the world will know my shame,
And yet if I keep silent I am lost.

Enter SOUSE.

SOUSE I went into the village, like you said,
In search of guests to join you in the feast;
The trouble is, the village isn't there,
Or what of it that's there is not much good,
Unless it's charcoal that you're after, Boss.
ASHBURNINGHAM (*Strangling with rage*) *What do you mean —*
SOUSE   I mean, that it's not there!
It seems, to save the place from rebel hands,
Your men were forced to burn it to the ground.
ASHBURNINGHAM *What do you mean by coming back like this — !*
SOUSE Begob, I came as quickly as I could.
ASHBURNINGHAM Prepare to die, you dog!
SOUSE   Now, hang on, Boss —

ASHBURNINGHAM *draws his sword, makes a
feint at* SOUSE, *who dodges the blow.*

What's wrong, for God's sake, what is it I've
done?
ASHBURNINGHAM It's not five minutes past since you refused
To open up the gate to my own house,
But left me standing out here, like a fool,
And poured down torrents of abuse on me.
SOUSE How's that? You sent me off to fetch the
guests —

ASHBURNINGHAM What guests?

SOUSE   The ones you wanted here for
          lunch,
     To help you celebrate your homecoming.

ASHBURNINGHAM I sent for guests — ? For lunch — ? To
          celebrate — ?

SOUSE That's right, after Her Ladyship and you
     Was reconciled.

ASHBURNINGHAM (*Aside*)   Oh, this gets worse and worse,
     This labyrinth in which I've lost my self.

ASHBURNINGHAM *bangs loudly on the gate.*

Come out, you damned usurper! Show
     yourself!

Scene Seven

Enter JUPITER *in the form of* ASHBURNINGHAM.

JUPITER Who is it out here knocking at my gate?
    (*To* ASHBURNINGHAM) Well, my good fellow,
      what is it you want?
ASHBURNINGHAM Almighty God! Who are you?
SOUSE   Holy Lord!
    I'm seeing double — two Ashburninghams!
JUPITER This really is most tiresome. Souse, come here.
    What of those guests I sent you off to fetch?

> SOUSE *can only gape at him in mute astonishment.*

> (*Aside*) It seems that I must round them up
>   myself.

> ASHBURNINGHAM *brandishes his sword.*

ASHBURNINGHAM (*To* JUPITER) Enough of your insults — come,
    draw your blade!

> SOUSE *looks from man to god and back again,
> then makes his choice, and goes and stands
> beside* JUPITER.

SOUSE (*To* ASHBURNINGHAM) Now listen here, imposter,
    watch your step.
ASHBURNINGHAM Can you not see the real imposter, Souse?
SOUSE (*Looking at* ASHBURNINGHAM) I can; that's who
    I'm looking at right now.
    A servant knows his master. (*Points to* JUPITER)
    Here he is.
    I've been his man this fifteen year and more,
    I'd know his voice and carriage anywhere.

ASHBURNINGHAM Out of my way, I'll run the villain through!

JUPITER My good man, calm yourself. Such violence
As this is wholly inappropriate.
I will observe, that someone so concerned
About his name must doubt his title to't.

SOUSE A good point, Boss! I see what he has done,
He's tricked himself all up to look like you,
But any fool just needs to look at him
To see he's nothing like you — not a bit!

ASHBURNINGHAM You traitor, Souse! I'll have you thrashed for
that.

SOUSE Oh, no you won't; (*To* JUPITER) he won't, ain't
that right, Boss?

ASHBURNINGHAM (*To* SOUSE) Old friend, you surely don't believe
these lies!
You see me humbled here, you see me robbed;
My name, my house, my table, yes, my bed,
This brute has tried to take away from me.

SOUSE If so, begob, then he's done more than *tried*.

JUPITER There is a way to put this to the test.
Why don't we ask the people to decide?

ASHBURNINGHAM What people?

JUPITER   Those that I have summoned
here.

ASHBURNINGHAM Oh, yes? And who are they, and where?

JUPITER   Why, there!

*He lifts his hand and casts a thunderbolt, and
immediately the house lights come on;* SOUSE
and ASHBURNINGHAM *gape at the audience.*

ASHBURNINGHAM Good God — !

SOUSE (*Wonderingly*) Have youse crowd been here all
along?

ASHBURNINGHAM *strides to front stage,
addresses the audience; the house lights
begin gradually to fade back to darkness.*

ASHBURNINGHAM Good people, listen, for I need your help.
I am only a soldier, it is true;
I have no way with words, no cunning tricks
By which to pull the wool over your eyes.
I do not understand what's happened here.
That creature you see standing at my gate
Is some foul spirit sent up out of Hell
To take from me the things that once were
    mine.
He wants to drive me out of hearth and home,
Out of my wife's affections, and the world's
Remembrance — yes, and even out of my
Own consciousness! Don't let him do it!
    Please!
Just look at me, and tell them who I am.
You know me; I'm that same Ashburningham
Who saved your houses and your fields from
    ruin,
Who met that rebel scum on Vinegar Hill
And taught them to respect our good King's
    rule.
Come, now, I beg you, say it: Who am I?

    Pause.

JUPITER I think their silence speaks their choice for
    them.
ASHBURNINGHAM (*To audience*) You damned ungrateful herd of
    Irish swine!

    House lights back to darkness.

JUPITER And now, if you'll excuse me for a while,
I must away to lunch, with my dear wife —
But here she is!

    Enter MINNA *and* KITTY.

    My darling, come, your hand.

JUPITER *takes* MINNA *by the hand and leads her forward.*

MINNA There was such a commotion that I came —
(*She sees* ASHBURNINGHAM) Oh, God in
Heaven, who is this I see!
JUPITER Who does it look like, dear?
MINNA He looks like you!
No, *more* than like: it is another you!
ASHBURNINGHAM My dearest Minna, tell them who I am!
MINNA (*To* JUPITER) Oh, Percy, please keep him away
from me!

ASHBURNINGHAM *rushes forward, tries to take*
MINNA*'s hand from* JUPITER*'s grasp.*

ASHBURNINGHAM My darling — !
MINNA No! Don't touch me!
ASHBURNINGHAM Minna!
Please!

He falls back in anguish.

MINNA (*To* JUPITER) Tell me, sir, the meaning of all this.
JUPITER He claims that he is me; what do you think?
ASHBURNINGHAM My dearest, please, my life depends on you.
JUPITER Which is your real husband?
KITTY Lady, speak!
JUPITER You are the only one who can decide.

MINNA *looks imploringly at* JUPITER.

The truth, child, come, in truth say which it is.

Pause.

MINNA How could there be a doubt? Of course, it's you.
SOUSE That's good enough for me. (*To* ASHBURNINGHAM)
Now, off you go!

67

ASHBURNINGHAM *runs forward, falls to one knee and this time succeeds in taking* MINNA's *hand.*

ASHBURNINGHAM Ah, Minna dearest, don't forsake me now!

MINNA *recoils from him.*

MINNA Let go of me, you lying, odious brute!
How dare you claim to be whom you are not,
When my real husband's standing by my side!
How could I be deceived by your disguise,
When you crept up and kissed me here last
    night?
How could I think your mean and peasant
    looks
(*Points to* JUPITER) Bore any likeness to *this*
    countenance?
To think, that I submitted to your lies,
And let you fawn on me, and fondle me,
Allowed my senses answer to your touch —
Oh, God, I cannot bear the memory!

JUPITER (*To* ASHBURNINGHAM) There now: am I
    Ashburningham, or not?

ASHBURNINGHAM If she says you are he, then so you are,
To her; I've never known my love to lie.

JUPITER Then kneel, and ask for her forgiveness.

ASHBURNINGHAM   No.
It's I that must forgive, and so I do.
It is a bitter lesson I have learned.

JUPITER What lesson's that?

ASHBURNINGHAM   Why, what it is to love.
It's all forgiveness, nothing more than that.
(*To* MINNA) My dear, I don't pretend to
    understand
These things that happened here. I know I've
    lost —
Lost you, lost love — I've even lost my self —
But all of it I forfeit, willingly,

68

If thereby I can give you happiness.

MINNA, *moved, begins to doubt.*

MINNA (*To* JUPITER) His voice, your voice — they
    sound so much alike.
JUPITER Of course they do; I borrowed mine from him.
MINNA You borrowed — ?
JUPITER   Yes.
MINNA   But how?
JUPITER   Oh, easily.
MINNA And last night, which of you — ?
JUPITER   Yes, it was I;
    As I am everywhere, and everywhen;
    For I am Jupiter.
KITTY   He's *what*? He's *who*?
SOUSE A god, he says, begod!

JUPITER *casts another thunderbolt, and*
MERCURY *swoops down from the flies, winged,*
and bearing the caduceus.

MERCURY (*With heavy sarcasm*)   You called, my lord?
ASHBURNINGHAM I don't pretend to know what's going on,
    But sir, if you expect me to believe —
MERCURY (*To* JUPITER) Shall I — ?

JUPITER *shrugs;* MERCURY *steps forward, touches*
a fingertip to ASHBURNINGHAM's *breast.*

ASHBURNINGHAM   O God!

He seems to suffer a heart attack, and collapses.

JUPITER (*To* MINNA)   Do you still
    doubt me, child?

MINNA *rushes to* ASHBURNINGHAM *and holds*
his head on her lap.

69

MINNA My darling, darling! (*Turns on* MERCURY)
       You — you've killed him!
JUPITER (*Gently*)   No.

> JUPITER *gestures to* MERCURY, *who leans down,*
> *touches his finger to* ASHBURNINGHAM'S
> *temple, immediately reviving him.*

MINNA (*To* JUPITER) How can you be a god, and yet
       love *me*?
JUPITER Perhaps what I love's your humility.

> *Pause.*

My child, I have mistreated you, I fear;
Your innocence is a rebuke to me.
I wanted you to love me — foolish hope —
I hoped that you would love me for myself;
Not as a god, but as I might have been,
Had I been mortal (*Points to* ASHBURNINGHAM)
    like this good man here.
That's what we envy, your mortality.
I tried to find in you a way to live,
When what I really want to do is die.
I had no right to toy with your poor heart.

> *Pause.*

All this you will forget, when I have gone —
(*To all the mortals*) So will you all, your
    memory wiped clean —
(*To* MINNA) But you've been tainted with
    divinity,
And from that you will never quite be free.
There will be certain days in summer when,
In sunstruck groves, or walking by the sea,
You'll feel my presence near you, hear my
    voice;
You'll think you have imagined it, and yet,

Inside you there will be an answering call.
Some April evening, when the rain has
　　ceased,
Your heart will shake, though you will not
　　know why;
You'll weep for nothing, pine for what's not
　　there.
For you, this life will never be enough,
Since there will always be an emptiness
Where once *I* was —

MINNA　You make me feel afraid, I'm trembling, look.

> ASHBURNINGHAM *rises, puts his arms around her.*

ASHBURNINGHAM　(*To* JUPITER) I beg you, please don't take her
　　from me.

JUPITER　　　　　No,
She's yours, for, Heaven knows, she's proved
　　her love.

> *Pause.*

And now I must away; great matters call.
Come, Mercury, let's leave them to their lives.

> JUPITER *strides toward the wings, his steps strong, all lethargy fallen from him. The mortals freeze, and stand like statues.*

MERCURY　(*To audience*) See how he strides, as strong as
　　ever was?
It's always this way, when he lets them go.
Debilitating business, being in love;
It puts a hundred thousand years on him,
The fond old fool.
(*To* JUPITER)　　Well, Father, and what now?
What battle shall we visit next? I hear
There'll be a good one soon at Waterloo.

71

Those Flanders fields were made for fighting
on —

JUPITER I'm going home to Heaven; satisfied?

MERCURY I know that Heaven's second best, compared
To this (*With a contemptuous wave*) bright
world of beauty, hope and joy.

JUPITER It's warmer, though, than our cold, lifeless
Heaven.

MERCURY And what about these people?

JUPITER (*Carelessly*)   Let them wake.

> MERCURY, *with malicious smile, approaches*
> ASHBURNINGHAM, *puts an arm about his*
> *shoulder;* ASHBURNINGHAM *remains frozen*
> *and impassive.*

MERCURY There's something, by the way, that he forgot
To mention, which I'm sure you'd like to know.
(*Whispers*) *Your wife's with child.*

JUPITER   What are you
doing! Come!

> MERCURY *swoops up into the flies.* JUPITER,
> *still standing by the wings, looks at* MINNA,
> *raises his hand in a blessing, then casts a*
> *thunderbolt, in the smoke of which he disappears.*
> *The mortals blink, waking from their trance.*

KITTY (*To* SOUSE) Well, don't just stand there — !

SOUSE   Eh — ?

ASHBURNINGHAM (*To* MINNA)   My darling!

MINNA   Ah!

Curtain.